HELP ME —
I'M WORRIED!

HELP ME —
I'M WORRIED!

Overcoming Emotional Battles
With the Power of God's Word

by

Joyce Meyer

Harrison House
Tulsa, Oklahoma

HELP ME – I'M WORRIED!
Overcoming Emotional Battles
With the Power of God's Word
ISBN 1-57794-010-5
Copyright © 1998 by Joyce Meyer
Life In The Word, Inc.
P. O. Box 655
Fenton, Missouri 63026

Published by Harrison House, Inc.
P. O. Box 35035
Tulsa, Oklahoma 74153

Contents

≈

Introduction

God wants to make a trade with you. He wants you to give Him all your cares, your problems, your failures — your "ashes" — and He will give you beauty. He will take your cares, and for them, He will care for you.

Humble yourselves therefore under the mighty hand of God, that he may exalt you in due time:

Casting all your care upon him; for he careth for you.

1 Peter 5:6,7 KJV

The Spirit of the Lord God is upon me, because the Lord has anointed and qualified me....To grant [consolation and joy] to those who mourn in Zion — to give them an ornament (a garland or diadem) of beauty instead of ashes ["beauty for ashes" KJV]....

Isaiah 61:1,3

God wants to take care of us, but in order to let Him, *we* must stop taking the care.

Many people want God to take care of them while they are worrying or trying to figure out an answer instead of waiting for God's direction. They are actually wallowing around in their "ashes," but still want God to give them beauty. In order for God to give us the beauty, we must give Him the "ashes."

We give Him our cares by trusting that He can and will take care of us. Hebrews 4:3 says: "For we who have believed (adhered to and trusted in and relied on God) do enter that rest...."

We enter into the Lord's rest through believing. Worry is the opposite of faith. Worry steals our peace, physically wears us out and can even make us sick. If we are worrying, we are not trusting God, and we are not entering God's rest.

What a great trade! You give God ashes, and He gives you beauty. You give Him all your worries and concerns, and He gives you protection, stability, a place of refuge and fullness of joy — the privilege of being cared for by Him.

Part 1

Dwelling in the Secret Place

1

~

Abiding in Protection

He who dwells in the secret place of the Most High shall remain stable and fixed under the shadow of the Almighty [Whose power no foe can withstand].

Psalm 91:1

God has a secret place where we can dwell in peace and safety.

The secret place is the place of rest in God, a place of peace and comfort in Him. This secret place is a "spiritual place" where worry vanishes and peace reigns. It is the place of God's presence. When we spend time praying and seeking God and dwelling in His presence, we are in the secret place.

The word *dwell* means "to make one's home; reside; live."[1] When you and I *dwell in*

Christ or *dwell in the secret place,* we do not just visit there occasionally, we take up permanent residence there.

In the New Testament, one of the Greek words translated *dwell* is the same Greek word translated *abide* in John 15:7 NKJV where Jesus says, "If you abide in Me, and My words abide in you, you will ask what you desire, and it shall be done for you."

If you and I abide in God, it is the same thing as dwelling in God. As a matter of fact, *The Amplified Bible* translates John 15:7, "If you live in Me [abide vitally united to Me] and My words remain in you and continue to live in your hearts, ask whatever you will, and it shall be done for you."

In other words, we need to be firmly planted in God. We need to know the Source of our help in every situation and in every circumstance. We need to have our own secret place of peace and security. We need to rely on God and trust Him completely.

In the Secret Place

> He who dwells in the secret place
> of the Most High shall remain stable
> and fixed....

Psalm 91:1

The psalmist says that he who dwells in the *secret place* will be settled and secure.

The secret place is a hiding place, a private place, or a place of refuge. It is the place we run to when we are hurting, overwhelmed or feeling faint. It is the place we run to when we are being mistreated or persecuted, when we are in great need or when we feel we just cannot take it anymore.

I remember when I was a child we lived in a large, roomy house. (My mother cleaned that house, and that was how we got our rent.) It was a huge, very ornate building with a number of wood carvings, and it had some neat little secret places in it. One day I found one of those little secret places. It was a small bench carved out underneath one of the stairwells with a stained glass window by it.

Even now I can still picture myself sitting on that bench just pondering. I don't know what I was pondering as a small child, but I do know I had quite a few hurts and problems.

My home life was marked by many upsetting and disturbing domestic situations. That carved-out place with a bench in the stairwell was like a hiding place for me. It was where I would go when I was afraid or needed comfort.

This verse tells us that God wants to be our hiding place.

Some people in the world use alcohol as their hiding place. Some use drugs and others television. Some just get depressed and pull the covers up over their head. There are a lot of people out there hiding from a lot of things.

Instead of looking to the world to hide us, God wants us to find our hiding place in Him. That is what is meant by the phrase "the secret place of the Most High." When we have problems, when we are in trouble, God wants us to take refuge under the protective shadow of His wings. He wants us to run to Him!

Under the Shadow of the Almighty

...under the shadow of the Almighty [Whose power no foe can withstand].

Psalm 91:1

If we are in the secret place of the Most High, where will we be found? According to the psalmist, we will be abiding "under the shadow of the Almighty." This is the place God wants His people to live.

Our heavenly Father does not want us just to visit Him once in a while or run to Him when we feel overwhelmed, He wants us to dwell under the shadow of His wings, to abide there, to live there. When we do that, we remain stable and fixed because no foe can withstand the power of the Almighty. If we remain in that place, the devil can do us no harm.

There was a time in my life when I just ran in and out of the secret place, but I have since found that when I go there and stay, when I abide there, I don't feel so overwhelmed.

We need the Lord all the time — not just occasionally. In John 15:5 Jesus says, "...apart from Me [cut off from vital union with Me] you can do nothing."

What exactly does it mean to abide under the shadow of the Almighty? First of all, a *shadow* implies "shade," a place of protection from the hot sun or from the heat of the world. A shadow, as we know, always has a border. If we intend to stay under the shadow of God's wings, there are definite borders within which we must stay.

A *border* is an intermediate area or boundary between two qualities or conditions. In the case of a shadow, a border is where the shade stops and the sunshine starts.

Suppose it is noon, the sun is out in full force, and we see a big tree. If we go and stand under that tree, we are going to be a lot more comfortable in the shade than if we continue to stand out in the sun.

When people work outdoors in the sun and begin to sweat, they like to find a shade tree to get under when break time comes. Some people plant shade trees around their house because it lowers the temperature of the interior of the house and makes it even cooler. So the shade is a desirable place to be, especially on a hot day.

If we decide to stay in the shade under the shadow of God's wings, life is going to be more comfortable. It is not going to be so hot, and we are not going to be "sweating it out," so to speak. Instead of worrying about our problems, we will be resting in God.

If we decide to stand in the sun, we are going to be uncomfortable, sweaty, miserable, thirsty and dry. It is up to each of us to decide where we are going to stand — in the shade (trusting God) or in the sun (sweating it out) — in Jesus, or in the world with all its problems.

Where will you decide to stand? I want to stay in the shade. But, as we all tend to do from time to time, I sometimes wander out of the shade and end up back out in the heat where the conditions are not too nice. Then when I am about to expire, I run back to the shade to get rested up again. Then eventually, I once more venture back out into the heat of the sun.

Romans 1:17 KJV says we can live from faith to faith. However, sometimes we live from faith to doubt to unbelief and then back to faith.

What if we really want to stay within the protection of the shadow but sometimes find ourselves outside of it? How will we know when we are getting out from under God's protection? We will know by the signposts the Lord has placed along our way.

2

~

Read the Signposts: Trusting God

Imagine you are driving down a road. This road is the road of life. In the middle of the road are lines. Sometimes there are double yellow lines that warn, "If you cross these lines, you are going to be in trouble; you run a high risk of a head-on collision."

Sometimes there are broken white lines meaning, "You can cross into the other lane and pass the car in front of you if you would like. If you cross these lines, you will probably be okay, but you can get into trouble if you do not watch the oncoming traffic to make sure the way is clear."

There are also roadside signposts that provide a specific direction or warning: "Soft Shoulder," "Falling Rocks," "Deer Crossing," "One Way," "Detour," "Under Construction,"

"Curve Ahead." If you heed the instructions on these signposts, they will help you keep your car on the road. You will avoid going too far to the left and getting into a collision or too far to the right and running into a ditch.

In the same way, in life there are spiritual signposts as well. In order to stay under God's protection, we must heed these signposts along the way that tell us to trust Him and not to worry, fear or be anxious, that tell us to cast our care on Him. Then instead of excessively trying to reason out a solution, we need to turn our thoughts to things that are "true," "honest," "just," "pure," "lovely," of "good report," of "any virtue" or of any "praise" (Philippians 4:8 KJV).

If we will heed these signposts and stay within the borders of the road, we will be able to remain on course. We will be protected and will experience in our lifetime the fulfillment of all the wonderful, marvelous promises of God's Word.

Heed the Signpost!

And your ears will hear a word
behind you, saying, This is the way;
walk in it, when you turn to the right
hand and when you turn to the left.

Isaiah 30:21

Suppose you are driving along the road of
life, and you begin to veer off the road to the
right. You notice that the road seems a little
more bumpy than it had been, and you begin
to pay closer attention to where you are
driving. Just then, you remember a signpost
a few miles back that said, "Trust God and
Don't Worry."

If you decide to continue on your course,
you will go even farther off the shoulder of
the road and could end up in the middle of
the ditch. Then you will have to call a tow
truck to come get you out.

So it is when we decide to worry rather
than trust God. We get out from under His
protection so the enemy is able to get at us

more easily. When that happens, we inevitably lose our peace.

Straight Paths

And cut through and make firm and plain and smooth, straight paths for your feet [yes, make them safe and upright and happy paths that go in the right direction]....

Hebrews 12:13

When you make a wrong decision, when you decide to worry rather than trust God, you will begin to get uncomfortable and start to lose your peace. You may even begin to get a sense that things are not working out right anymore and that you have missed the way somewhere.

As soon as you lose your peace, you need to stop and say, "Wait a minute. What am I doing wrong?"

Sometimes as I am going down life's road I suddenly realize that deep down inside I am not at peace. When that happens I stop and say, "Lord, where did I go wrong?" I know that when I lose my peace, it is an indication that I have traveled out from under the protection of the shadow of His wing.

Usually it will be because I have started worrying. Sometimes it will be because I have done something wrong and have not repented or because I have mistreated somebody and have not been sensitive to my mistake.

In that situation I simply ask Him, "Lord, show me why I have lost my peace." Once I know that, I can take the necessary steps to get the situation back in order.

If you find you are having a worry attack as you follow through on what the Lord has shown you to do, I suggest that you read aloud the words of Jesus in Matthew 6:25-32.

Stop Worrying

> Therefore I tell you, stop being perpetually uneasy (anxious and worried)

about your life, what you shall eat or what you shall drink; or about your body, what you shall put on. Is not life greater [in quality] than food, and the body [far above and more excellent] than clothing?

Matthew 6:25

If you are on a diet, perhaps you should start by reading the first part of that verse — the part about eating and drinking! If you are like me, when you are dieting, it seems that all you can think about is food!

I remember when I used to go on a diet. All day long I would be thinking about when and what I was going to eat and how I was going to fix it. I would be mentally weighing it out and calculating how many calories were in it. Often it would even make me more hungry because all I was doing was thinking about food!

Actually, we probably worry less about what we are going to eat and drink than we do about what we are going to do in a particular situation: what if this happens or what if that happens? Most of us have enough clothes, adequate food, comfortable houses and serviceable cars. But when things get tough, and we are faced with situations that seem impossible, we have voices within our mind that scream, "What are you going to do now?" And we begin to worry.

Look at the Birds

> Look at the birds of the air; they neither sow nor reap nor gather into barns, and yet your heavenly Father keeps feeding them. Are you not worth much more than they?
>
> *Matthew 6:26*

Have you ever seen a bird sitting in a tree having a nervous breakdown? Have you ever seen a bird pacing back and forth saying to himself, "Oh, I wonder where my next worm is coming from? I need worms! What if God quits making worms today? I don't know what I would do. Maybe I would starve to death! What if God keeps making worms, but they aren't juicy this year or what if He doesn't send any rain, and no worms come out of the ground? What if I can't find any straw to build my nest?" What if, what if, what if!

Jesus said, "Look at the birds!" They aren't having a nervous breakdown. Every morning they are flying around outside just singing and having a good time.

I wonder how much peace you and I could enjoy if we would just take off an hour or so and go watch the birds!

What Does Worry Accomplish?

And who of you by worrying and being anxious can add one unit of measure (cubit) to his stature or to the span of his life?

Matthew 6:27

Of course, the answer is no one. But we can surely shorten our life span if we insist on continuing to make worry a habit!

Instead of worrying, we need to be more like the birds of the air who are totally dependent upon the Lord to feed them and yet who sing all day long as though they didn't have a care in the world.

Consider the Lilies

And why should you be anxious about clothes? Consider the lilies of the field and learn thoroughly how they grow; they neither toil nor spin.

Yet I tell you, even Solomon in all his magnificence (excellence, dignity, and grace) was not arrayed like one of these.

But if God so clothes the grass of the field, which today is alive and green and tomorrow is tossed into the furnace, will He not much more surely clothe you, O you of little faith?

Matthew 6:28-30

What Jesus was saying was that the flowers of the field do not get all "hung up" in works of the flesh. They don't work at being lilies; they just are. And God dresses them very nicely.

Do we really think we are any less important to God than birds and flowers?

Don't Be Anxious

Therefore do not worry and be anxious, *saying,* What are we going to have to eat? or, What are we going to have to drink? or, What are we going to have to wear?

For the Gentiles (heathen) wish for and crave and diligently seek all these things, and your heavenly Father knows well that you need them all.

Matthew 6:31,32

The problem with worry is that it causes us to start *saying* — things like: "What are we going to have to eat? What are we going to have to drink? What are we going to have to wear?" In other words, "What are we going to do if God doesn't come through for us?"

We begin to fret and fuss with the words of our mouth. Instead of calming our fears and removing our worries, that just makes them even more deeply ingrained.

The problem with this way of doing things is that it is the way people act who don't know they have a heavenly Father. But you and I do know we have a heavenly Father, so we need to act like it. Unbelievers may not know how to rely on Him, but we should.

Jesus assures us that our heavenly Father knows all the things we need before we ask Him. So why should we worry about them? Instead, we need to focus our attention on the things that are much more important — the things of God.

Seek First Things First

But seek (aim at and strive after) first of all His kingdom and His righteousness (His way of doing and being right), and then all these things taken together will be given you besides.

Matthew 6:33

For many years I would pace around before going in to minister in one of my meetings, getting myself all worked up. I would be praying, "Oh, God, help me!" There is nothing wrong with praying for God's help, but I was praying more out of anxiety than out of faith.

Now while preparing to minister, I simply study and prepare the best I can. Then just before the meeting begins I spend time in quiet prayer and meditation, worshipping the Lord and fellowshipping with Him.

Never once has He told me to seek a big meeting. Never once has He told me to seek a big offering. All I do is seek Him, and He takes care of the size of the crowd, the amount of the offering, and everything else.

Too often we spend all of our time seeking God for answers to our problems when what we should be doing is just seeking God.

As long as we are seeking God, we are staying in the secret place, under the shadow of His wing. ("...under His wings shall you trust and find refuge..." Psalm 91:4.) But when we start seeking answers to all the problems and situations that confront us, trying to fulfill our desires rather than God's will, we get out from under the shadow of His wing.

For many years I sought God about how I could get my ministry to grow. The result was that it stayed just the same as it was. It never grew. Sometimes it even went backwards. What I didn't realize was that all I needed to do was to seek the Kingdom of God, and He would add the growth.

Do you realize that you don't even have to worry about your own spiritual growth? All you need to do is seek the Kingdom, and you will grow. Seek God, abide in Him and He will cause increase and growth.

A baby just drinks milk and grows. All you and I have to do is to desire the sincere milk of the Word, and we will grow. (1 Peter 2:2.)

We can never experience any real measure of success by our own human effort. Instead, we must seek first the Kingdom of God and His righteousness; then all these other things we need will be *added* to us.

We are not to seek God's presents, but His presence.

Spend Time in the Shade

One thing have I asked of the Lord, that will I seek, inquire for, and [insistently] require: that I may dwell in the house of the Lord [in His presence] all the days of my life, to behold and gaze upon the beauty [the sweet attractiveness and the delightful loveliness] of the Lord and to meditate, consider, and inquire in His temple.

For in the day of trouble He will hide me in His shelter; in the secret place of His tent will He hide me; He will set me high upon a rock.

And now shall my head be lifted up above my enemies round about me; in His tent I will offer sacrifices and shouting of joy; I will sing, yes, I will sing praises to the Lord.

Psalm 27:4-6

Sometimes we live our lives backwards. This is exactly what I was doing some years ago. I was seeking a big ministry. I was seeking all kinds of changes in myself because I didn't like myself. I was seeking for my husband to change. I was seeking for my children to change. I was seeking healing and prosperity. I was seeking everything under the sun, and I was not spending any time in the shade.

Then the Lord stepped in and showed me what I was doing wrong. He used Psalm 27:4-6 to emphasize to me that I must first seek Him and His presence all the days of my life.

At that time, I was asking for a lot of things, none of which had much to do with God's presence. Yet as I began to seek Him, that is exactly what I began to desire more of. Then when troubles came, He hid me, as it were, in the secret place of His tent. When the enemy came against me to try to destroy me, I lifted up shouts of joy and sang praises to the Lord.

The devil could not get to me because I was in the secret place of the Most High. I was inaccessible to him. Satan could not cause me to have a nervous breakdown because I was in the shade where I was anxious for nothing.

Be Anxious for Nothing

Be anxious for nothing, but in everything by prayer and supplication, with thanksgiving, let your requests be made known to God; and the peace of God, which surpasses all understanding, will guard your hearts and minds through Christ Jesus.

Philippians 4:6,7 NKJV

A long time ago, God told me that when I came to Him in prayer I was to give to Him whatever the devil had tried to give to me.

That is what prayer is. The devil comes to us and hands us a problem. We say, "I can't carry this because it's too heavy for me. Here, God, I give it to You."

In Philippians 4:6, 7 the apostle Paul tells us in essence, "Pray and *don't* worry." He doesn't say, "Pray *and* worry." When we pray and give our problems to God, that is a sign to the Lord that we are trusting Him. That is what prayer is supposed to be.

I have to do this quite often where my teenaged son Danny is concerned. He is still at home, and because the ministry my husband and I are in requires that we travel, it grieves my heart sometimes to have to leave Danny behind. Before he graduated, he once told me on the telephone that he had experienced some struggles in school and that he missed us when we were gone, especially in the morning when he got up and when he went to bed at night.

Through the years, Dave and I have developed a really good relationship with our son. We love him, and he loves us. (Our next youngest was ten years old when God spoke to us to have Danny, so he is our baby!) We were concerned about him as he faced high school and the pressures and influences we knew he would encounter there.

All of us are faced with daily challenges which must be dealt with. Falling into the trap of feeling sorry for ourselves, walking around with our head hanging down because everything in our life is not working out perfectly, will not get us anywhere. We must change our focus and do what the Bible says — pray!

Every time I started to worry about Danny while we were away from him ministering, I prayed:

Father, I thank You that You are taking care of Danny. Thank You, Lord, that You have a good plan for his life and that You are watching over him and working out everything for the best for him. Thank You that he is covered by the blood of Your Son Jesus.

When you and I start praying that way, the devil will leave us alone. He will see that we will not be shaken and that we are determined to trust God.

Stay in the Positive

Only it must be in faith that he asks with no wavering (no hesitating, no doubting). For the one who wavers (hesitates, doubts) is like the billowing surge out at sea that is blown hither and thither and tossed by the wind.

For truly, let not such a person imagine that he will receive anything [he asks for] from the Lord.

James 1:6,7

If we take our concerns to the Lord in prayer and then continue to worry about them, we are mixing a positive and a negative force. Prayer is a positive force, and worry is a negative force. If we add them together, we come up with zero.

I don't know about you, but I don't want to have zero power, so I try not to mix prayer and worry.

God spoke to me one time and said, "Many people operate with zero power because they are always mixing the positives and the negatives. They have a positive confession for a little while, then a negative confession for a little while. They pray for a little while, then they worry for a little while. They trust for a little while, then they worry for a little while. As a result, they just go back and forth, never really making any progress."

Why not make a decision to stay in the positive by trusting God and refusing to worry?

3

~❧~

Everything's Going To Be All Right

The second signpost deals with anxiety. It says, "Fear Not and Don't Be Anxious." This signpost has a warning that is similar to the first, "Trust God and Don't Worry," but the consequences of disobeying it are a bit more drastic. Instead of going in a ditch, as you would if you were to veer to the right, you run the risk of having a head-on collision. It is like crossing over that center double yellow line while taking a curve.

Anxiety, unlike worry, is an uneasy feeling that lingers even after we think we have dealt with it. It is almost like a double portion of worry. Once we go in this direction we step out of faith and into fear, especially fear of tomorrow and fear of the unknown. The result is anxiety.

Signs of Anxiety

> Anxiety in a man's heart weighs it down....
>
> *Proverbs 12:25*

Anxiety brings a heaviness to a person's life.

Webster says that *anxiety* is "a state of being uneasy, apprehensive, or worried...."[1] Sometimes this uneasiness is really vague, something we just cannot put our finger on. We may not even know exactly what it is. All we know is that we are uneasy, sometimes even around other people.

According to Webster, *apprehension* is "an anxious feeling of foreboding; dread."[2] In other words, apprehension is a bad case of anxiety.

I remember a bad case of anxiety I once had. I had experienced so many bad things in my life that I finally got to the point that I expected bad things to happen. But I really didn't understand what I was experiencing until the Lord revealed it to me in Scripture.

Evil Forebodings

All the days of the desponding and afflicted are made *evil* [by anxious thoughts and *forebodings*], but he who has a glad heart has a continual feast [regardless of circumstances].

Proverbs 15:15

One morning, many years ago, I was fixing my hair in front of the mirror. I sensed a vague feeling that something bad was going to happen to me. I didn't understand what it was at the time because I had only been filled with the Holy Spirit and studying the Word of God for a short while. All I knew was that I had a vague feeling of being threatened.

So I decided to ask the Lord, "What is this thing that hangs around me all the time? It has been with me as far back as I can remember." The Lord told me it was "evil forebodings."

Never having heard that term, I thought to myself, "What in the world is a 'foreboding'?" So I went and looked it up in the dictionary. I discovered that a *foreboding* is "a sense of impending misfortune or evil."[3]

I learned that a foreboding has nothing to do with anything that is happening right at the moment; it is a negative feeling about the outcome of some event in the future.

At the time, I didn't know that term was in the Bible. Later, however, I came across it in Proverbs 15:15 which speaks of "anxious thoughts" and "evil forebodings."

God wants us to get rid of evil forebodings so that we can enjoy life. But that is easier said than done because Satan, our adversary, wants us to believe that nothing is ever going to turn out right for us. He wants us to believe that we will always be misunderstood and unappreciated, that nobody will ever like us or want to be around us, that nobody will ever care anything about us. He wants us to feel humiliated about the past, helpless about the present and hopeless about the future. He wants to heap so much worry and anxiety upon us that we will be drawn away from our relationship to God and distracted from accomplishing the work He has set before us.

Each of the meanings of the word *anxious* — "worried and distressed about an uncertainty," "attended with, exhibiting, or producing worry" — confirms this fact.[4]

If You're Redeemed, Say So!

Let the redeemed of the Lord say so, whom He has delivered from the hand of the adversary.

Psalm 107:2

Once you realize that the devil is trying to distract you, don't just sit around and let him beat you up with worry and negative thoughts. Open your mouth and say something he doesn't want to hear, and he will leave. Begin to confess your authority in Christ.

Sometimes while I am preparing to speak at a church or seminar, negative thoughts will begin to bombard me.

Some years ago I was wondering how many people had registered in advance for a ladies' meeting I was scheduled to lead. When I asked my assistant, she said that not many had registered but that the organizers of the meeting believed there would be as many in attendance as the previous year.

All of a sudden the thought flashed across my mind, "What if nobody comes? What if my team and I travel all of that distance and only a few people show up?" Then I encouraged myself with my own mouth and said out loud, "Everything is going to be all right."

Sometimes we have to do that because if we don't, those evil forebodings will continue to hang around to cause us worry and anxiety.

Once I recognized those anxious thoughts and evil forebodings and took authority over them, God began to bring some deliverance to my life so I could start to enjoy it.

Satan places anxious and worried thoughts in our minds, sometimes actually "bombarding" our minds with them. He hopes we will receive them and begin "saying" them out of our mouths. If we do, he then has material to actually create the circumstances in our lives he has been giving us anxious thoughts about.

Words have creative power in the spiritual realm. Genesis 1:3 says, "God *said,* Let there be...and there was..."!

Jesus said, "Therefore take no thought, *saying,* What shall we eat? or, What shall we drink? or, Wherewithal shall we be clothed?" (Matthew 6:31 KJV). If we take a negative thought and start saying it, then we are only a few steps away from real problems. "Take therefore no thought for the morrow: for the morrow shall take thought for the things of itself..." (v. 34 KJV).

Enjoy Life!

> ...a gentle and peaceful spirit...[is not anxious or wrought up, but] is very precious in the sight of God.
>
> *1 Peter 3:4*

Anxiety also means "care," "concern," "disquietude," "a troubled state of mind."[5] Peter tells us that the type of spirit God likes is a peaceful spirit, not one that is anxious or wrought up.

When we are wrought up, we are all tense inside, and we feel as though our stomach is tied in knots. Everything becomes a burden to us — a big, intense, overwrought deal — so that we are not able to relax and enjoy life as God intends.

In my case, I was always tense and upset because my childhood had been stolen through abuse. (At a very early age, I was already feeling like an adult.) Because I never really got to be a child, I didn't know how to let go and be childlike. So when I got married and had children of my own, I didn't know how to truly enjoy them.

For years I couldn't even enjoy my husband because I was too intense about trying to change him. I was continually trying to perfect him — and everybody else.

I had children, but I didn't enjoy them. Each day before they left for school, I made sure that every hair was in place, that there was not a wrinkle in their clothes, and that their lunch was securely packed away in their lunch box. I loved my children, but I didn't enjoy them.

I had a nice house, I kept it spotlessly clean with everything in its place, but I didn't enjoy it. Nobody else enjoyed the house either. We couldn't live in it. All we could do was look at it.

My children had nice toys, but they didn't enjoy them because I wouldn't let them. I didn't want them to get their toys out and play with them.

I never knew what fun was. Whatever it was, I didn't think it was anything my family was entitled to. I figured, "You don't *need* to have fun. All you *need* is to put in a good day's work."

I remember telling my kids, "Get out of here and go play." Then when they did so, I would come right along behind them saying, "Pick up that mess! Get that stuff cleaned up right now! All you ever do around here is make messes!"

What I needed to realize at that point in my life was that if things did not turn out exactly the way I wanted them to, it was not the end of the world. I needed to learn to relax and enjoy life.

The Bible says in Psalm 118:24 NKJV, "This is the day the Lord has made; we will rejoice and be glad in it."

In John 16:33, Jesus said, "I have told you these things, so that in Me you may have [perfect] peace and confidence. In the world you have tribulation and trials and distress and frustration; but be of good cheer [take courage; be confident, certain, undaunted]! For I have overcome the world...."

In Philippians 4:4 the apostle Paul says, "Rejoice in the Lord always [delight, gladden yourselves in Him]; again I say, Rejoice!"

Don't be so intense. Lighten up a little. Give God a chance to work. Make the decision to enjoy life.

Changed From Glory to Glory

And all of us, as with unveiled face, [because we] continued to behold [in the Word of God] as in a mirror the glory of the Lord, are constantly being transfigured into His very own image in ever increasing splendor and from one degree of glory to another; [for this comes] from the Lord [Who is] the Spirit.

2 Corinthians 3:18

Do you realize that if the only time you decide to enjoy yourself is when everything is perfect, you are never going to have much fun?

Don't make the mistake of waiting to enjoy yourself until you and everyone around you are all perfected and have arrived at the finish line.

The Bible says that you and I are being changed into God's own image and are going from glory to glory. That means we are going to go through a lot of different stages. We need to learn how to enjoy the glory of the stage we are in right now while we are moving into the next one. We must learn to say, "I'm not where I need to be, but, thank God, I'm not where I used to be. I'm somewhere in the middle, and I'm going to enjoy each stage."

When our children are babies they do cute things like smile and coo, but they also do things that are not so cute like cry in the middle of the night, cut teeth, and get diarrhea. We catch ourselves saying, "I'll be glad when they get through this stage so I can really enjoy them."

Somehow they make it through that stage, then they enter the next one. At this point, they are talking and saying cute expressions, but they are also walking and throwing any object they can get their hands on. Again we find ourselves wishing they were through this stage.

Soon they are in kindergarten, and we find ourselves saying, "I'll be glad when they're in the first grade, then they'll go to school all day." But as soon as they are in elementary school, we start saying, "I'll be glad when they start high school." Then when they graduate from high school, we say, "I'll be glad when they're grown and married."

Then one day that happens, and suddenly we realize that we never enjoyed any stage of their lives. We were always waiting to be glad *when*.

That is the way I used to spend my entire life. I was always going to be glad some other time.

When I used to hold meetings of fifty people, I would think, "I'll be so glad when hundreds of people start coming to my meetings." The truth is that when that finally happened, it didn't make me any happier.

Every phase we go through brings with it a certain amount of joy, but it also comes with its own little set of problems. What we need to do is to learn to be glad in spite of any circumstance.

Be Glad in Spite of Circumstances

> For You, O Lord, have made me
> glad by Your works; at the deeds of
> Your hands I joyfully sing.
>
> *Psalm 92:4*

Some years ago I finally found the doorway to happiness. It is found in the presence of God.

I used to be happy if God was doing something that made me glad. But I didn't know how to be glad *because* of Him. I knew how to seek His hand, but I didn't really know how to seek His face.

Don't think you are going to be glad when God does the next thing for you that you want Him to do. As soon as He does, there is going to be something else you are going to want that you think you can't be glad until you get. Don't spend all your life waiting until some other time to be happy.

One day after I had received this breakthrough, I was going to a meeting, and I was singing that once popular spiritual song, "You have made me glad, You have made me glad; I will rejoice for You have made me glad." It was then that the Holy Ghost spoke to me and said, "For the first time, you're singing that song right."

Because God hears our hearts more than our words, that song sounded different to Him. Before, what He heard was, "The things You have done for me have made me glad, the things You have done for me have made me glad; I will rejoice for all the things You have done for me have made me glad."

When the Lord was doing what I wanted Him to do for me, I was glad, but when He wasn't doing what I wanted Him to do for me, I was not glad. So I lived an "up-and-down" life. It was like riding a roller coaster. I was getting worn out from going up and down all the time. If my circumstances suited me, I was up, and if they didn't, I was down.

If we are to live in the fullness of joy, we must find something to be glad about besides our circumstances.

Be Glad in Spite of People

Be glad in the Lord and rejoice, you [uncompromisingly] righteous [you who are upright and in right standing with Him]; shout for joy, all you upright in heart!

Psalm 32:11

Even if every one of our circumstances suits us, we will eventually find that the world is full of people who don't suit us. As soon as we shape up the ones who don't suit us, still others will come along who don't suit us. It is an unending cycle.

In our ministry, we have a large number of people on our staff. Even though they are some of the most wonderful people I have ever met, there are times when they don't all make me glad.

Even being around Christian people will not make us glad all the time. The only One Who can make us glad all the time, every time, is Jesus — and even He cannot do that for us unless we allow Him to do so.

The Martha Syndrome

Now while they were on their way, it occurred that Jesus entered a certain village, and a woman named

Martha received and welcomed Him into her house.

And she had a sister named Mary, who seated herself at the Lord's feet and was listening to His teaching.

But Martha [overly occupied and too busy] was distracted with much serving; and she came up to Him and said, Lord, is it nothing to You that my sister has left me to serve alone? Tell her then to help me [to lend a hand and do her part along with me!]

Luke 10:38-40

No one knew the Source of happiness, peace and joy better than Mary, the sister of Martha. When their guest, Jesus, arrived in their home, she positioned herself at His feet so she could hear everything He was going to say without missing a word. She was excited that He had decided to visit them that day and wanted to really enjoy the time they would have together. So she sat right down and fixed her eyes on Jesus.

Then there was her sister — dear old Martha. She had already spent all day running around cleaning and polishing and cooking, trying to get everything ready for Jesus' visit.

(The reason I find it so easy to picture Martha in this situation is because I used to be just like her.)

Everything had to be in order when Martha's guest arrived. Once He did arrive, she busied herself in the kitchen getting all the food prepared and putting the last minute touches on the table setting.

Eventually Martha got upset and came to Jesus saying in so many words, "Master, why don't You make my sister Mary get up and help me do some of the work around here?" Hoping to get some sympathy and perhaps a little recognition for all she had done, she was shocked when He said, "Martha, Martha, you are anxious and troubled about many things; there is need of only one or but a few things. Mary has chosen the good portion... which shall not be taken away from her" (Luke 10:41,42).

I am sure things got a bit quiet around the house after that comment. But the truth is, Martha needed to hear it.

I remember one time when God said something similar to me. He said, "Joyce, you can't enjoy life because you're too complicated." And He was right! I could complicate a simple barbecue!

I remember one time when I saw some of our friends and on the spur of the moment invited them to come visit. I remember saying something like, "Hey, why don't you guys come over Sunday? We'll throw some hot dogs on the grill and open a bag of potato chips and a can of pork and beans. I'll make some tea, and we'll just sit around the patio and have a good time, or maybe we can play some ball or some games or something."

After I said this, I was feeling good thinking about how much fun we were going to have. I got in my car and started to drive home. By the time I got back to the house, the hot dogs had turned into steaks, and the potato chips had turned into potato salad! After all, I wouldn't want my friends to think I could only afford hot dogs or that I didn't know how to make potato salad.

It wasn't long before I decided that the barbecue grill needed to be painted and the old lawn furniture needed to be replaced. Of course, the lawn needed to be mowed and the house thoroughly cleaned. After all, I had to make a good impression on my guests.

After a while, I started thinking about not only the six people I had invited but the fourteen who would get offended if they knew the six were there and I had not asked them also. So now, all of a sudden, this simple get-together had become a nightmare. I was giving in to the fear of man.

Then the Martha syndrome sank in a little more. I began madly cleaning the house and mopping the floors. I was sending everybody out to the store to get this and that. Invariably, I got mad at Dave and the kids and said something like, "I just don't understand why it is that I have to do *all of the work* around here while everybody else just has fun!" By that time, I had "Martha" written all over my face, and I knew that, unlike Mary, I had not chosen the best portion.

Live in the Now

Beloved, we are [even here and] *now* God's children; it is not yet disclosed (made clear) what we shall be [hereafter], but we know that when He comes and is manifested, we shall [as God's children] resemble and be like Him, for we shall see Him just as He [really] is.

1 John 3:2

In reality, it is the choices we make today that determine whether we will enjoy the moment or waste it by worrying. Sometimes we end up missing the moment of today because we are too concerned about tomorrow.

Another definition of *anxiety* is "Uneasiness and distress about future uncertainties."[6] The definition that God gave me follows along the same lines: "Anxiety is caused by trying to mentally or emotionally get into things that are not here yet (the future) or things that have already been (the past)."

One of the things that we need to understand is that God wants us to learn how to be *now* people. For example, 2 Corinthians 6:2 KJV says, "...Behold, now is the day of salvation" and Hebrews 4:7 says, "...Today, if you would hear His voice and when you hear it, do not harden your hearts."

We need to learn to live now. Too many times we spend our mental time in the past or the future. This may sound a little comical to you, but I have had so many problems with this tendency in my life that God once revealed to me that I was in anxiety even when I was brushing my teeth!

While I was brushing my teeth, I was already thinking about the next thing I wanted to do. I was in a hurry, and my stomach was already tied in knots.

When you and I don't really give ourselves to what we are doing at the moment, we become prone to anxiety. Brushing our teeth may seem a simplistic matter, but I believe that is exactly the kind of everyday situation that often gives us the most problems.

I can remember when I was first baptized in the Holy Spirit. My mind was such an awful mess that I had trouble with the most ordinary things of life. I would get up in the morning, get my three little kids off to school and my husband off to work, and then start in on what I needed to get done that day. But I couldn't keep my mind on anything.

I would be in the bedroom making my bed when all of a sudden I would realize I hadn't loaded the dishwasher. So I would rush into the kitchen to do that, leaving the bed only partially made.

As I was loading the dishwasher I might think, "You know, I really need to go downstairs and get the meat out of the freezer so it will thaw in time for dinner."

So I would rush downstairs to get the meat out of the freezer. As I did so I might see the dirty laundry piled up and decide I really needed to stop and get it into the washer.

Just then I might think of a phone call I needed to make and would run back upstairs to attend to that chore. In the midst of all that rush and confusion I might suddenly remember I needed to go to the post office and get some bills in the mail. So off I would hurry to do that errand.

By the time the day was over, I had a worse mess than I had when I started out. Now everything was half done, and I was frustrated and worn out. Why? Simply because I never gave myself totally to one thing.

One Thing at a Time

> Keep your foot [give your mind to what you are doing]....
>
> *Ecclesiastes 5:1*

Do you know why we don't give ourselves to one thing? Because we are too concerned with getting on to the next thing. We need to do what the writer of Ecclesiastes has told us to do — keep our mind on what we are doing at the moment. If we don't do that, we will lose our footing or balance in life, and nothing will make any sense!

We must make a decision to live in the now, not in the past or the future, because getting into yesterday or tomorrow when we should be living in today causes us to lose our anointing for today. We have to take one day at a time because that is the only way we are going to get where we are going.

We live in such an instant society that we want somebody just to wave a magic wand over us and make everything all better. But things just don't happen that way. Change comes one day at a time.

One Day at a Time

...do not worry or be anxious about tomorrow, for tomorrow will have worries and anxieties of its own. Sufficient for each day is its own trouble.

Matthew 6:34

In John 8:58 Jesus referred to Himself as "I AM." If you and I, as His disciples, try to live in the past or the future, we are going to find life hard because Jesus is always in the present. That's why He told us not to be concerned about yesterday or tomorrow.

If we try to live in the future or the past, life is going to be hard. But if we will live in the now, we will find the Lord there with us. Regardless of what situations life brings our way, He has promised never to leave us or forsake us but to always be with us and help us. (Hebrews 13:5; Matthew 28:20.)

Giving ourselves to one thing at a time in the now is not just a physical matter, it is a mental and emotional matter as well. For example, we can be standing in one place physically, but be having a conversation with someone in our mind someplace else.

When we go on to the next thing mentally, it creates unnecessary pressure upon us. When we do come back to the present, we may not be clear as to what went on while we were mentally absent.

That is why the devil constantly tries to snatch our minds away and take us off somewhere else. He wants us to miss out on what is happening in the now.

I remember one time when I was angry about something my husband had done. In those days, I would get mad and stay mad for days. Finally Dave said something that really got my attention: "Wouldn't it be pitiful if Jesus came tonight, and you had spent your last day on earth like this?" That gave me something to think about.

You and I don't need to be anxious about tomorrow when we have all we can handle today. Even if we manage to solve all our problems today, tomorrow we will just have more to deal with, and even more the next day.

Why waste time being anxious when it is not going to solve anything? Why be anxious about yesterday which is gone or tomorrow which has not yet arrived? Live in faith now. Fear not and don't be anxious.

4

God's Thoughts Are Higher Than Our Thoughts

Are you always trying to figure everything out? Many of us have fallen into that ditch. Instead of casting our care upon the Lord, we go through life carrying every bit of it.

When we are trying to figure everything out, we are exalting our reasoning above God's thoughts and plans for our life. We are placing our ways higher than His ways.

Second Corinthians 10:5 tells us that we should "...lead every thought and purpose away captive into the obedience of Christ...." The third signpost is "Cast All Your Care and Avoid Reasoning." When we do that, we will stop trying to figure everything out and learn to cast our care upon the Lord and enter into His rest.

Enter God's Rest

> For we who have believed (ad-
> hered to and trusted in and relied on
> God) do enter that rest....

> *Hebrews 4:3*

This passage refers to the Children of Israel entering the land of Canaan rather than wandering in the desert. But we can apply it to our lives: if we are not resting, then we are not really believing and trusting, because the fruit of belief and trust is rest.

Sometimes I am tempted to try to figure out every detail of what's happening or the reason things are happening. But I know that when I do that I am not really trusting God.

In Proverbs 3:5 we are told, "Lean on, trust in, and be confident in the Lord with all your heart and mind and do not rely on your own insight or understanding." In other words, we are told, "Trust God and don't try to figure things out on the basis of what you see," not, "Trust God while you are trying to figure everything out!"

I realized that with my mouth I had been telling God I trusted Him while in my mind I was still trying to figure out everything for myself. What Proverbs 3:5 tells us to do is to trust in the Lord with all of our heart and all of our mind!

That means we must give up excessive reasoning.

Reasoning Contrary to the Truth

> But be doers of the Word [obey the message], and not merely listeners to it, betraying yourselves [into deception by *reasoning* contrary to the Truth].
>
> *James 1:22*

When God revealed to me that I had to give up excessive reasoning, it was a real challenge to me because I was addicted to it. I couldn't stand it if I did not have everything figured out.

For example, God told us to do some things in our ministry several years ago that I didn't have the slightest idea how to go about doing. One of those things was going on television on a daily basis. Of course, that multiplied the workload and financial responsibility of the ministry by five. It required more employees and more space.

But God never called me to figure out exactly how to accomplish everything He asked me to do. He called me to seek *Him,* not the answer to my problems, then obey what He tells me to do.

I didn't know where to get the money to do all the things God told us to do, or the space or the people. But I have had enough experience with God to know that if I will just stay in the shade, under the shadow of His wing, worshipping and praising Him, taking my part of the responsibility but casting my care on Him, He will bring everything to pass in accordance with His will and plan.

My part of the responsibility is to do whatever He shows me to do. All He asks of me is to say, "I'm going to start taking steps, Lord, and I believe You are going to provide." But I can assure you that God is never going to ask me to worry or to try to figure out how He is going to do everything He is leading me to do.

When we worry, we lose our peace, and when we try to figure everything out, we fall into confusion. Staying in peace is abiding under the shadow of the Almighty!

One time I asked the Lord, "Why are we all so confused?" He answered by saying, "If you will stop trying to figure things out, then you won't be confused."

The beginning of confusion is a signpost warning that we are about to take a wrong turn and get into trouble.

Confusion is the result of reasoning with our own understanding when we should be trusting in the Lord with all our heart to make the way for us according to His plan. When we trust that His thoughts are higher than our thoughts, we can stop confusion before it starts.

Endless Conversations

...do not be anxious [beforehand] how you shall reply in defense or what you are to say.

For the Holy Spirit will teach you in that very hour and moment what [you] ought to say.

Luke 12:11,12

Sometimes we not only try to figure out ahead of time what we ought to *do,* we also try to figure out what we ought to *say.*

At home you may be needing to confront your spouse about some issue between the two of you. At work you may be needing to ask your boss for a raise or reprimand an employee about his inappropriate behavior. Whatever the situation may be that is facing you right now, you may be full of anxiety.

Why not make a decision to trust God instead of planning and rehearsing a conversation over and over in your head? Why not simply believe God wants you to deal with what is placed in front of you without figuring out ahead of time what you are going to say?

You may want to have a general idea of what you need to present, but there is a balance to be maintained. If you become obsessive and keep going over the situation in your head, that is a sign you are not depending upon the anointing of the Lord. You are depending on yourself, and you are going to fail.

Do you know that you and I can say a few words under God's anointing and bring peace and harmony, or we can say two hundred words in our own flesh and cause total havoc and confusion?

Sometimes we rack our brains trying to come up with a plan to handle a difficult situation. Once we think we have finally decided just what we are going to do, the troubling thought pops into our head, "Yes, but what if...?" And we end up more confused than ever.

I remember one night lying in bed mentally dealing with a situation that was causing me to be restless. Eventually I found myself in one of those endless imaginary conversations: "If I say this, they will say that. If that happens, I'm going to get upset! Then what am I going to do?"

I knew I had to discuss some unpleasant things with some people I didn't want to offend, and I knew it wouldn't be easy. Even though I didn't want those involved to be angry with me, I also didn't want to shirk my responsibility by being a "menpleaser."

(Ephesians 6:6 KJV; Colossians 3:22 KJV.) I needed a sense of peace and confidence about the matter.

God's peace is always available — but we must choose it. We must choose to stand either in the hot sun of worry — and be sweaty, miserable, thirsty and dry — or in the cool, comforting shade of God's peace.

God's Plans for Us Are Good!

> For I know the thoughts and plans that I have for you, says the Lord, thoughts and plans for welfare and peace and not for evil, to give you hope in your final outcome.
>
> *Jeremiah 29:11*

Because of my abusive home environment as a child I learned to make sure that everything I said was just right before I opened my mouth to speak. I was afraid if I said the wrong thing, I would be made to suffer for it.

I spent many years of my life outlining conversations in my head in order to make sure that everything was going to sound just right. Eventually, of course, my mind developed the habit of thinking negatively and defensively.

Because of my insecurities and my fear of being rejected, I would spend days trying to figure out the meaning of some casual remark made to me by someone who had meant nothing by it.

God doesn't want us using our minds that way. It is a useless waste of time. Our heavenly Father has a plan for our life. His thoughts are above our thoughts, and His ways are above our ways. (Isaiah 55:8,9.) Neither you nor I will ever figure Him out.

After struggling for years, I finally said to the Lord, "What is my problem?" The Lord spoke something to me then that changed my life. He said, "Joyce, because of the way you were raised, fear is embedded in your thinking processes."

Of course, the Lord had been working with me from the time I was filled with the Holy Spirit to root that fear out of me. Even though I had come a long way, I realized I still had a long way to go.

Despite all that, He said to me, "Joyce, everything is going to be all right!" When He said that, it was like a breakthrough. It reminded me of what I used to say to my kids when they would come to me upset and crying: "It's okay! Mama will fix it. Everything is going to be all right." Even though the message was simple, I have reminded myself of it on countless occasions.

I remember one time in particular when my ministry team and I were scheduled to hold a seminar. Although we had re-ordered the tape labels we needed for the seminar, we had worked our way down to the last one. When we called the company, it appeared the order had been lost. Even though we had sent the order in plenty of time initially, now we had run out of time, and we had to put in a special rush order.

The day after the new shipment date, the labels still had not arrived! Instead of allowing that situation to get to me, I simply said, "Everything is going to be all right." Sure enough, by the time I got home, the people at the office had called to tell me that the labels had arrived right after I left the office.

Developing Trust

...we glory in tribulations also: knowing that tribulation worketh patience;

And patience, experience; and experience, hope.

Romans 5:3,4 KJV

How many times have you frustrated yourself and gotten all upset needlessly over these kinds of situations? How many years of your life have you spent saying, "Oh, I'm believing God. I'm trusting God," when, in reality, all you were doing was worrying, talking negatively and trying to figure out everything on your own? You may have thought you were trusting God because you were saying, "I trust God," but inside you were anxious and panicky. You were trying to learn to trust God, but you were not quite there yet.

Do I mean that developing trust and confidence is simply a matter of saying, "Don't worry; everything will be all right"? No, I don't. Trust and confidence are built up over a period of time. It usually takes some time to overcome an ingrained habit of worry, anxiety and fear.

That is why it is so important to "hang in there" with God. Don't quit and give up, because you gain experience and spiritual strength every round you go through. Each time you become a little stronger than you were the last time. Sooner or later, if you don't give up, you will be more than the devil can handle.

Only God Can Really Help

...You are He Who took me out of the womb; You made me hope and trust when I was on my mother's breasts.

I was cast upon You from my very birth; from my mother's womb You have been my God.

Be not far from me, for trouble is near and there is none to help.

Psalm 22:9-11

I have been walking with God now for a long time, so I have some experience behind me and have been through some hard times. But I have never forgotten the many years the devil controlled and manipulated me. I remember the nights I used to spend walking the floor crying, feeling like I just couldn't make it.

I remember running to my friends and others I thought might be able to help me. Eventually I got smart enough to stop running to people — not because I didn't like them or trust them, but because I knew they really could not help me, only God could.

I heard one speaker say, "If people can help you, you don't really have a problem."

I used to get so aggravated at my husband because when he would be having problems or going through rough times, he wouldn't tell me about it. Then two or three weeks after he had won the victory, he would say, "I was really going through a rough time a few weeks ago."

Before he would finish, I would ask, "Why didn't you tell me?"

Do you know what he would say?

"I knew you couldn't help me, so I didn't even ask!"

I am not saying it is wrong to share with someone you love and trust what is going on in your life, but Dave understood a truth that I needed to put into practice in my own life. There are times that only God can help. Although I would have liked to be able to help my husband, I really couldn't. Only God could, and he needed to go to Him.

The Lord once told me that we need to learn how to suffer privately. One of the verses He gave me along this line is Isaiah 53:7 NKJV, "He was oppressed and He was afflicted, yet He opened not His mouth...." Once you reach a certain point in your walk with God, this is one of the golden rules for gaining even more strength in Him.

Cast All Your Care Upon the Lord

Casting all your care upon Him,
for He cares for you.

1 Peter 5:7 NKJV

In my walk with the Lord, I wanted to get to the point where I had stability, did not worry, was not full of unnecessary reasoning and could cast all my care upon Him.

My husband has a special gift in this area. He has been through a lot with God, and over the years the Lord has given him a real sense of peace and security. (It is a good thing because I was such a worrier that if we had both been like me, we never would have made it.)

I was the household bookkeeper and took care of paying the bills. Every month I would get out the calculator and begin adding up all the bills. I would work myself into a frantic mess worrying about how we were going to pay them all.

Dave, on the other hand, would be in the family room playing with the kids. They would be putting rollers in his hair and crawling all over his back while they all watched television. I would hear them giggling and laughing and having a great time.

Pretty soon I would get mad at Dave because he was enjoying life while I was so miserable.

But that is the way it goes. When we are miserable, we get angry at anybody who won't be miserable with us.

I would be out in the kitchen wringing my hands and saying, "Oh, dear God, I trust You. I believe You are going to come through for us again this month." I was saying the right words, but I was worried and miserable.

The end of the month would come, and, sure enough, God would do a miracle in our finances. Then, of course, I would have the next month to worry about. Even though I knew we were right in the middle of the will of God, I would still worry.

Trusting God is one of those areas in which we have to get experience for ourselves. It doesn't come by going through a prayer line or having hands laid on us. It isn't something someone else can give us. We have to get it for ourselves over a period of time.

Cry Out to God

> Be merciful and gracious to me, O
> Lord, for to You do I cry all the day.
>
> *Psalm 86:3*

But finances are not the only area in which I have had to learn to trust God. There have been times in my life when I have hurt so badly that I have lain on my office floor and held onto the legs of the furniture to keep from running away from God. I have had to stretch out on my face and cry out to Him, "Lord, You have *got* to help me. If You don't do something, I can't hang on any longer."

It is in desperate times like that we get to know God really well. To be honest, crying out to the Lord like a little child and depending totally on Him is healthy. When we cry out, we don't have to worry about how we sound or how pretty we look.

I am sure that there have been times in my life when I looked like an absolute idiot as I cried out to the Lord, but I did it anyway.

In Which Direction Are You Headed?

...I have learned how to be content (satisfied to the point where I am not disturbed or disquieted) in whatever state I am.

Philippians 4:11

Don't get discouraged with yourself if you are not quite where you would like to be. It takes time and experience to learn how to cast all your care upon the Lord and stay under His shadow in the secret place.

The question is not, "Where are you right now?" Instead, the question is, "In which direction are you headed?"

Are you learning? Are you willing to change? Are you open to grow? The very fact that you are reading this book right now indicates that you are serious about overcoming fear, anxiety and insecurity. Now all you need to do is to get some experience in casting all your care upon the Lord so that you can avoid vain reasoning.

Fulfill Your Responsibility
But Cast Your Care

Roll your works upon the Lord [commit and trust them wholly to Him; He will cause your thoughts to become agreeable to His will, and] so shall your plans be established and succeed.

Proverbs 16:3

I think the reason that I have always tried to figure everything out is because of my lifelong fear of failure. I have always been a responsible person, and I have always wanted things to turn out right. But in addition to the responsibility that I took, I also took the care.

God wants us to *fulfill our responsibility,* but *cast our care.* Why does He want us to cast our care? Because He *cares* for us.

I don't know about you, but I spent too many years of my life tormenting myself with worry and anxiety, trying to handle things that I could not handle or trying to handle things that were not mine to handle. As a result, years of my life were wasted.

If you want to be really frustrated, just go around all the time trying to do something about something you can't do anything about. If you do, it is going to frustrate you unbearably.

"Oh, Well"

> Cease from anger and forsake wrath; fret not yourself — it tends only to evildoing.
>
> *Psalm 37:8*

Whenever I find myself in a situation that I can't do anything about, I have found that a good way to cast my care upon the Lord is simply to say, "Oh, well."

Take, for example, the morning that Dave spilled his orange juice in the car and got a little of it on my sweater. Immediately he said, "Devil, I'm not impressed." And I said,

"Oh, well." So that problem was solved, and we pressed forward with the rest of our day.

Some things just aren't worth getting upset about, yet many people do. Unfortunately a large majority of Christians are upset, fretful and full of anxiety *most* of the time. It is not the big things that get to them; it is the little things that don't fit into their plans. Instead of casting their care and just saying, "Oh well," they are always trying to do something about something they can't do anything about.

On more occasions than one, that simple phrase "Oh, well" has really helped me to make it through.

One time our son Danny made a mistake at the very end of a paper he was writing for homework. So he crumpled up his paper and proceeded to start all over again. Eventually he ended up getting mad and upset and wanted to give up all together.

So his father and I began to work with him about just saying, "Oh, well." It worked.

After that when he was tempted to give up, we said, "Danny," and he would say, "Oh, well." Then he would go back to whatever he was doing and complete it.

Be Well-Balanced

Be well balanced....

1 Peter 5:8

Sometimes in trying situations our anxiety gets in the way of our doing what we should. All we can do is our best, then trust God with the rest.

We function best when we have a calm, well-balanced mind. When our mind is calm, it is without fear, worry or torment. When our mind is well-balanced, we are able to look the situation over and decide what to do or not to do about it.

Where most of us get in trouble is getting out of balance. Either we move into a state of total passivity in which we do nothing, expecting God to do everything for us, or we become hyperactive, operating most of the time in the flesh. God wants us to be well-balanced so that we are able to face any situation of life and say, "Well, I believe I can do certain things about this situation, but no more."

This happens to many of us at income tax time. We think we have paid in enough throughout the year to meet our tax obligation. Then we find out that we still owe money. The time is usually short, and we don't know how to get the money the government demands.

Instead of getting distraught and full of fear and worry, we need to go before God and say, "Well, Lord, I'm believing You to help me in this situation, but is there something You want me to do?"

God may show us to take a part-time job for a while to earn what we need to pay off our taxes. He may show us a way to borrow the money, along with a plan to pay it back quickly. Whatever it is that God shows us to do about our problem, we need to be diligent enough to do it. Then we need to trust Him with the outcome.

Sometimes we think we should be doing more than we are to solve our problems or meet our needs. But if we rush ahead without getting God's direction, we will be acting in the flesh, and all our efforts will be in vain. Sometimes we just have to make a determination to rest even though our mind is yelling, "What are you going to do?"

We must be confident that the God we serve does not require us to do more than we know how. Once we have done all we know to do, we can trust God with the rest. That is what I call faith and balance.

A Man of Faith and Balance

[Urged on] by faith Abraham, when he was called, obeyed and went forth to a place which he was destined to receive as an inheritance; and he went,

although he did not know or trouble
his mind about where he was to go.

Hebrews 11:8

Abraham was a man of faith and balance.
Think for a moment about his situation.

In obedience to the Lord, Abraham left
behind his family, his friends and his home to
set out on a journey to some unknown place.

I am sure that every step of the way the
devil was screaming in his ear, "You fool!
Where do you think you're going? What are
you going to do when night comes? Where
are you going to sleep? What are you going
to eat? Come on, Abraham, what are you
doing out here? What makes you think this
was God's idea anyway? Do you know of
anybody else God has told to do this?"

Don't Trouble Your Mind

And He said to them, Why are you
disturbed and troubled...?

Luke 24:38

Despite what the devil was screaming at him, Abraham went on. The Bible says that although he did not know where he was going, he did not *"trouble his mind"* about it! (Hebrews 11:8.)

Sometimes we trouble our own mind! Some of us love to worry so much that if the devil did not give us something to worry about, we would go dig something up!

Let's think about our mind for a moment. What is our mind supposed to be full of? It is supposed to be full of praise, full of the Word of God, full of exhortation and edification, full of hope and full of faith.

Now let's take a brief inventory of the thoughts we think throughout the day. It is sad to say, but most of us would have to admit that our mind is full of worry, fretfulness, fear, figuring, plotting, planning, theorizing, doubt, anxiety and uneasiness.

As a result, some of the gears of faith in our mind have cobwebs in them. We need to blow away those cobwebs and lubricate the gears of faith with the oil of the Holy Spirit — even though it may be hard when those gears of faith begin to roll again after so many years of disuse!

Like Abraham, we need to move out in faith and do what we can, then trust God with the rest and not trouble our mind about it. We need to get our faith in gear, but leave our mind at rest.

Don't waste your life. Determine what is your responsibility and what is not. Don't try to take on God's responsibility. Do what you can do, what He expects you to do, then leave the rest to Him. Fulfill your responsibility, but cast your care.

Conclusion

❧

Verse 2 of Psalm 91 carries a similar message to that of verse 1 which we examined earlier.

> He who dwells in the secret place of the Most High shall remain stable and fixed under the shadow of the Almighty [Whose power no foe can withstand].
>
> I will say of the Lord, He is my Refuge and my Fortress, my God; on Him I lean and rely, and in Him I [confidently] trust!
>
> *Psalm 91:1,2*

Our Refuge and Fortress

Both of these verses show us that we do not need to be worried, anxious or fretful because we can put our trust in God and place our confidence in Him.

But verse 2 not only says that God is our refuge, it also says that He is our fortress.

A refuge is different from a fortress. A refuge is a secret place of concealment in which the enemy cannot find us. If we are hidden in God, then Satan cannot locate us. We can see what is going on, but the devil cannot see us. He doesn't know where we are because we are hidden from his sight under the shadow of the Almighty.

A fortress, on the other hand, is a visible place of defense. The enemy knows we are there, but he cannot get to us, because we are inaccessible to him — as in the old Western movies in which the soldiers built a strong wooden fort as protection against their enemies.

We can either be in the hiding place where we see the enemy, but he doesn't see us, or we can be in a visible fort where the enemy plainly sees us but cannot get to us because we are surrounded by God's protection.

Verse 2 is just as important as verse 1 because the rich promises of this whole chapter are dependent upon the conditions of these two verses being met. "...He will give His angels [especial] charge over you to accompany and defend and preserve you in all your ways [of obedience and service]" (v. 11) if the conditions of verses 1 and 2 are met — if we are obedient to them.

Leaning on Him

For we have heard of your faith in Christ Jesus [the leaning of your entire human personality on Him in absolute trust and confidence in His power, wisdom, and goodness]....

Colossians 1:4

In verse 2 of Psalm 91 when the psalmist says, "I will *say* of the Lord," He is not just referring to lip service. "Saying of the Lord" does not mean just memorizing Scriptures and repeating them out loud. To "say of the

Lord" requires that we truly trust in Him, that we place our confidence totally in Him, that we lean on Him completely.

According to Colossians 1:4 that is really what faith is — the leaning of the entire human personality on God in absolute trust and confidence in His power, wisdom and goodness.

Some time ago the Lord showed me how we often lean on Him. Because of our fears, we lean somewhat on Him. But we keep enough weight on our own feet so that if God moves away, we will keep standing on our own.

We can tell when we are not really leaning on God because our thoughts will go something like this: "Yes, Lord, I trust You, but just in case You don't come through I have an alternative plan to fall back on."

That isn't trusting God totally and completely! God wants us to trust Him without reserve, with no thoughts or plans for failure.

Is the Lord really your refuge? Is He really your fortress? Do you really lean and rely on Him and trust in Him? Or are you just giving Him lip service?

If you have proven verses 1 and 2 for yourself, the rest of Psalm 91 is full of wonderful, marvelous promises for you.

He Will Deliver and Cover You

For [then] He will deliver you from the snare of the fowler and from the deadly pestilence.

[Then] He will cover you with His pinions, and under His wings shall you trust and find refuge; His truth and His faithfulness are a shield and a buckler.

Psalm 91:3,4

The first of these wonderful, marvelous promises are found in verses 3 and 4 which speak of the Lord's deliverance and protection.

Both the shield and the buckler are forms of protection used during combat. Often-times the shield was large enough to cover the whole body of a person, protecting him from the arrows of the enemy. Some shields were rounded rather than flat and offered more protection from arrows that might fly from the right or the left.[1]

The buckler, on the other hand, was a small shield worn on the arm or held by the hand. It was used more in hand-to-hand fighting and would provide all-around protection as the warrior turned to fight the enemy.[2] This is similar to the imagery found in Psalm 125:2 which says, "As the mountains are round about Jerusalem, so the Lord is round about His people...."

Regardless of the situation in which you and I may find ourselves, God is for us. It may seem hopeless to us, but if the Lord is for us, who can be against us? (Romans 8:31.)

The Lord is with us because He has promised, "...I will never leave you nor forsake you" (Hebrews 13:5 NKJV). He is under us because the Bible says that He upholds us with

His promise. (Psalm 119:116.) He is over us because we are told in Psalm 91:4, "...He will cover you with His pinions, and under His wings shall you trust and find refuge...."

Now get this picture firmly embedded in your mind. God is around you. He is for you. He is with you. He is under you, and He is over you. The devil is the only one who is really against you — and as long as you are dwelling in the secret place of the Most High, stable and fixed under the shadow of the Almighty, the enemy cannot find you or get to you!

If all this is true, why should you be afraid?

You Shall Not Be Afraid

You shall not be afraid of the terror of the night, nor of the arrow (the evil plots and slanders of the wicked) that flies by day,

Nor of the pestilence that stalks in darkness, nor of the destruction and sudden death that surprise and lay waste at noonday.

A thousand may fall at your side, and ten thousand at your right hand, but it shall not come near you.

Only a spectator shall you be [yourself inaccessible in the secret place of the Most High] as you witness the reward of the wicked.

Because you have made the Lord your refuge, and the Most High your dwelling place.

Psalm 91:5-9

You and I need to learn how to hide ourselves in God. If we can learn how to dwell in that secret place, then we can give the devil a nervous breakdown. We will be able to sit still and watch him try to get at us, but he won't be able to because we will be inaccessible to him.

Some years ago, God made a great transition in my life. At the time, I was already saved and baptized in the Holy Spirit, but I was still struggling and having a lot of problems. Then the Lord began to teach me that in His presence is fullness of joy and that the only way I would ever have any stability in my life was to dwell in His presence.

At that point in my life, I was so tired of the ups and downs that I yearned for stability. I didn't want to be an emotional mess. I didn't want to be controlled by my circumstances. I didn't want to spend the rest of my days screaming at the devil. I wanted to get on with my life and be able to receive and enjoy all the blessings the Bible said were mine as a child of God.

When I got to that point, the Lord started teaching me about dwelling in His presence. For years I studied all about it and more and more began to apply it in my life.

Now, years later, I can hardly begin to tell you what a transition there has been in my life. I have become so happy and so stable.

That doesn't mean that I never have problems. That doesn't mean that I never struggle. But it does mean that in the midst of the problems and struggles of life, I am able to stay in His presence and remain stable.

Psalm 91 is not just a nice piece of inspiring literature. It is true, and I can verify its truth with my own life.

If you will only learn to dwell in that secret place, then the devil will no longer have the upper hand over you. He will no longer have control over you.

When you have made the Lord your refuge and the Most High your dwelling place, you will be able to sit and watch the reward of the wicked, but no evil will befall you.

No Evil Shall Befall You

There shall no evil befall you, nor any plague or calamity come near your tent.

For He will give His angels [espe-
cial] charge over you to accompany
and defend and preserve you in all
your ways [of obedience and service].

They shall bear you up on their
hands, lest you dash your foot against
a stone.

Psalm 91:10-12

The Amplified Bible translation lays out so
clearly that this angel of protection is present if
we are walking in obedience and serving God.

One of the women who works for me was
sitting in a boat one day. She had just been
reading and confessing verse 10 about no
calamity coming near her tent because of
God's angelic charge over her. All of a
sudden, the boat hit a wave, she fell over, and
her head hit the side of the boat.

Then she was perplexed. She didn't
understand how she could be claiming and
confessing a verse of protection, then get
hurt. When she asked the Lord about it, He

said to her, "You aren't dead, are you?" Even though she may not have thought of it that way, His angels did protect her.

How many times do you think you might have been killed if God's angels had not protected you? Probably more times than you would like to even think about!

We don't need to be complaining about what we don't see God doing. We need to be thanking Him for what He *is* doing.

You Shall Tread on the Enemy

> You shall tread upon the lion and adder; the young lion and the serpent shall you trample underfoot.
>
> *Psalm 91:13*

Luke 10:19 NKJV is a cross reference to this verse and further explains what the lion, adder, scorpion and serpent represent: "Behold, I give you the authority to trample on serpents and scorpions, and over all the power of the enemy, and *nothing* shall by any means hurt you."

The lion, adder, serpent and scorpion all represent the enemy. God has given us the authority to trample or tread on them. The authority, *exousia,* that He has given to us is a "delegated authority" from Jesus to us.[3] If we choose to use it, we can tread on the enemy. That is our place in God when we assume our rightful position.

Because We Love Him

Because he has set his love upon Me, therefore will I deliver him; I will set him on high, because he knows and understands My name [has a personal knowledge of My mercy, love, and kindness — trusts and relies on Me, knowing I will never forsake him, no, never].

He shall call upon Me, and I will answer him; I will be with him in trouble, I will deliver him and honor him.

Psalm 91:14,15

Notice that in order to qualify for God's blessings and protection we must have a personal knowledge of His name. We cannot depend upon a relationship with God through our mother or father or friend. We must have a relationship with the Lord for ourselves. We must go to the hiding place, the secret place, and spend time there with God.

A lot of times all we think about is the "deliver me" part of this passage, and we say, "Deliver me, deliver me, deliver me." But deliverance is a process. When we have trouble, first of all, God will be *with* us in that trouble. He will strengthen us and take us through it victoriously. *Then* He will deliver us and honor us.

For many years, God was *with* me in the trials and troubles that I was going through while I was trying to overcome my past. But when He began to *deliver* me He also began to honor me.

When you have trouble, do you run to the phone, or to the throne? At first it may seem hard, but you need to come to the point in your life where you run to God and not to people when you are in trouble or a decision needs to be made. There is no reason to call up a bunch of people who barely know what they are doing in order to ask them what you should be doing.

Most of us have more than enough to do just trying to run our own lives without attempting to give advice to others.

Instead, learn to run to God. Learn to run to that secret place, that dwelling place, that hiding place. Learn to say, "Lord, nobody can help me but You. I am totally dependent upon You."

Many times, God will anoint somebody else to help us, but if we turn to others first, He is insulted. We need to learn to *go to God first* and say, "Lord, if You are going to use somebody to help me, You are going to have to choose and anoint that person because I don't want just anybody trying to tell me what to do. I want a word from You, or I don't want anything."

With Long Life

With long life will I satisfy him and show him My salvation.

Psalm 91:16

Sometimes it is easy to see that certain sins of the flesh such as alcoholism, drugs and sexual promiscuity, can lead to death. But we tend to soft pedal sins like worry, anxiety and reasoning. We rationalize them away saying that surely these are not sins. And yet they are. They too wear on our body and lead us to an early death through heart attack, ulcers or high blood pressure.

But God's plan for us is to be satisfied with long life and to experience the wonderful, marvelous promises of this psalm.

As you travel down the road of life, the next time you are attacked by the devil, put into practice the commands of Psalm 91:1 and 2 — dwell in the secret place of the Most High under the shadow of the Almighty, leaning on Him and making Him your refuge and your fortress.

Follow the Signposts

But after I am raised [to life], I will go before you....

Mark 14:28

So the signposts along the way are: (1) trust God and don't worry; (2) fear not and don't be anxious; (3) cast all your care and avoid reasoning.

In order not to veer off to the right or to the left, pay attention to these signposts. If you do find yourself veering to one side or the other, correct yourself to keep from getting into a collision or going off into a ditch.

On the Christian journey, one of the main reasons for veering off the road is worry. In John 15:5, Jesus said, "...apart from Me [cut off from vital union with Me] you can do nothing." Meditate on that verse and let the word *nothing* grip you. Worry can do *nothing* to change your situation. Instead the attitude of faith does not worry, fret and have anxiety concerning tomorrow; because faith understands that wherever it needs to go, Jesus has already been there.

It is not necessary to know and understand the reason behind everything that is going on in your life; trust that whatever you need to know, the Lord will reveal to you. Choose to be satisfied to know the One Who knows and does all things well.

Part 2

Scriptures

Scriptures
To Overcome Worry

❧

Read and confess the following Scriptures to help you live a worry-free life.

Anxiety in a man's heart weighs it down, but an encouraging word makes it glad.

Proverbs 12:25

All the days of the desponding and afflicted are made evil [by anxious thoughts and forebodings], but he who has a glad heart has a continual feast [regardless of circumstances].

Proverbs 15:15

You will guard him and keep him in perfect and constant peace whose mind [both its inclination and its character] is stayed on You, because he commits himself to You, leans on You, and hopes confidently in You.

Isaiah 26:3

Therefore I tell you, stop being perpetually uneasy (anxious and worried) about your life, what you shall eat or what you shall drink; or about your body, what you shall put on. Is not life greater [in quality] than food, and the body [far above and more excellent] than clothing?

Look at the birds of the air; they neither sow nor reap nor gather into barns, and yet your heavenly Father keeps feeding them. Are you not worth much more than they?

Matthew 6:25,26

Therefore do not worry and be anxious, saying, What are we going to have to eat? or, What are we going to have to drink? or, What are we going to have to wear?

Matthew 6:31

So do not worry or be anxious about tomorrow, for tomorrow will have worries and anxieties of its own. Sufficient for each day is its own trouble.

Matthew 6:34

...the cares and anxieties of the world and distractions of the age, and the pleasure and delight and false glamour and deceitfulness of riches, and the craving and passionate desire for other things creep in and choke and suffocate the Word, and it becomes fruitless.

Mark 4:19

Peace I leave with you; My [own] peace I now give and bequeath to you. Not as the world gives do I give to you. Do not let your hearts be troubled, neither let them be afraid. [Stop allowing yourselves to be agitated and disturbed; and do not permit yourselves to be fearful and intimidated and cowardly and unsettled.]

John 14:27

My desire is to have you free from all anxiety and distressing care....

1 Corinthians 7:32

Do not fret or have any anxiety about anything, but in every circumstance and in everything, by prayer and petition (definite requests), with thanksgiving, continue to make your wants known to God.

And God's peace [shall be yours... that peace] which transcends all understanding shall garrison and mount guard over your hearts and minds in Christ Jesus.

Philippians 4:6,7

...whatever is true, whatever is worthy of reverence and is honorable and seemly, whatever is just, whatever is pure, whatever is lovely and lovable, whatever is kind and winsome and gracious, if there is any virtue and excellence, if there is anything worthy of praise, think on and weigh and take account of these things [fix your minds on them].

Philippians 4:8

Casting the whole of your care [all your anxieties, all your worries, all your concerns, once and for all] on Him, for He cares for you affectionately and cares about you watchfully.

1 Peter 5:7

Prayer To Combat Worry

Father, help me not to worry. I realize worry does me no good, but in fact, only makes my situation worse. Help me keep my mind on good things that will benefit me and Your Kingdom.

Lord, I am thankful that You are taking care of me. You have a good plan for my life. I am going to start taking the steps You have shown me to take to fulfill that plan. I place my trust in You and in Your Word. I cast all my cares on You because I know that You care for me.

In Jesus' name, amen.

Prayer for a
Personal Relationship
With the Lord

❧

If you have never invited Jesus, the Prince of Peace, to be your Lord and Savior, I invite you to do so now. Pray the following prayer, and if you are really sincere about it, you will experience a new life in Christ.

Father,

You loved the world so much, You gave Your only begotten Son to die for our sins so that whoever believes in Him will not perish, but have eternal life.

Your Word says we are saved by grace through faith as a gift from You. There is nothing we can do to earn salvation.

I believe and confess with my mouth that Jesus Christ is Your Son, the Savior of the world. I believe He died on the cross for me and bore all of my sins, paying the price for them. I believe in my heart that You raised Jesus from the dead.

I ask You to forgive my sins. I confess Jesus as my Lord. According to Your Word, I am saved and will spend eternity with You! Thank You, Father. I am so grateful! In Jesus' name, amen.

See John 3:16; Ephesians 2:8,9; Romans 10:9,10; 1 Corinthians 15:3,4; 1 John 1:9; 4:14-16; 5:1,12,13.

Endnotes

Introduction

1 *Webster's New World College Dictionary,* 3rd ed., s. v. "dwell."

Chapter 3

1 *Webster's New World College Dictionary,* 3rd ed., s. v. "anxiety."

2 *Webster's,* 3rd ed., s. v. "apprehension."

3 *Webster's II New College Dictionary*, s.v. "foreboding."

4 *Webster's II,* s.v. "anxious."

5 *Webster's II,* s.v. "anxiety."

6 *Webster's II,* s.v. "anxiety."

Conclusion

1 Merrill F. Unger, *Unger's Bible Dictionary* (Chicago: Moody Press, 1966), p. 89.

2 Unger, p. 90.

3 James Strong, *The Exhaustive Concordance of the Bible* (Nashville: Abingdon

1890), "Greek Dictionary of the New Testament," p. 30, entry #1849, "delegated influence: — authority...."

About the Author

∼

Joyce Meyer has been teaching the Word of God since 1976 and in full-time ministry since 1980. As an associate pastor at Life Christian Center in St. Louis, Missouri, she developed, coordinated and taught a weekly meeting known as "Life In The Word." After more than five years, the Lord brought it to a conclusion, directing her to establish her own ministry and call it "Life In The Word, Inc."

Joyce's "Life In The Word" radio and television programs are heard or seen throughout the United States and the world. Her teaching tapes are enjoyed internationally. She travels extensively conducting Life In The Word conferences.

Joyce and her husband, Dave, business administrator at Life In The Word, have been married for over 33 years and are the parents of four children. All four children are married, and along with their spouses, work with Dave and Joyce in the ministry. Joyce and Dave reside in Fenton, Missouri, a St. Louis suburb.

Joyce believes the call on her life is to establish believers in God's Word. She says, "Jesus died to set the captives free, and far too many Christians have little or no victory in their daily lives." Finding herself in the same situation many years ago, and having found freedom to live in victory through applying God's Word, Joyce goes equipped to set captives free and to exchange *ashes for beauty*. Joyce believes that every person who walks in victory leads many others into victory.

Joyce has taught on emotional healing and related subjects in meetings all over the country, helping multiplied thousands. She has recorded more than 200 different audio-cassette albums and is the author of 34 books to help the Body of Christ on various topics.

Her "Emotional Healing Package" contains over 23 hours of teaching on the subject. Albums included in this package are: "Confidence"; "Beauty for Ashes" (includes a syllabus); "Managing Your Emotions"; "Bitterness, Resentment, and Unforgiveness"; "Root of Rejection"; and a 90-minute Scripture/music tape entitled "Healing the Brokenhearted."

Joyce's "Mind Package" features five different audio tape series on the subject of the mind. They include: "Mental Strongholds and Mindsets"; "Wilderness Mentality"; "The Mind of the Flesh"; "The Wandering, Wondering Mind"; and "Mind, Mouth, Moods & Attitudes." The package also contains Joyce's powerful 288-page book, *Battlefield of the Mind*. On the subject of love she has two tape series entitled, "Love Is..." and "Love: The Ultimate Power."

Write to Joyce Meyer's office for a resource catalog and further information on how to obtain the tapes you need to bring total healing to your life.

To contact the author write:

Joyce Meyer Ministries
P. O. Box 655
Fenton, Missouri 63026

or call:
(636) 349-0303

Internet Address:
www.jmministries.org

*Please include your testimony
or help received from this
book when you write.
Your prayer requests are welcome.*

To contact the author
in Canada, please write:

Joyce Meyer Ministries Canada, Inc.
Lambeth Box 1300
London, ON N6P 1T5

or call:
(636) 349-0303

In Australia, please write:

Joyce Meyer Ministries-Australia
Locked Bag 77
Mansfield Delivery Centre
Queensland 4122

or call:
(07) 3349 1200

Books by Joyce Meyer

How to Succeed at Being Yourself

Eat and Stay Thin

Weary Warriors, Fainting Saints

Life in the Word Journal

Life in the Word Devotional

*Be Anxious for Nothing —
The Art of Casting Your Cares
and Resting in God*

*The Help Me! Series:
I'm Alone!
I'm Stressed! • I'm Insecure!
I'm Discouraged! • I'm Depressed!
I'm Worried! • I'm Afraid!*

*Don't Dread —
Overcoming the Spirit of Dread with the
Supernatural Power of God*

*Managing Your Emotions
Instead of Your Emotions Managing You*

Life in the Word (Quotes)

Healing the Brokenhearted

"Me and My Big Mouth!"

Prepare to Prosper

Do It! Afraid

*Expect a Move of God in Your Life...**Suddenly***

*Enjoying Where You Are on the Way
to Where You Are Going*

The Most Important Decision You'll Ever Make

When, God, When?

Why, God, Why?

The Word, the Name, the Blood

Battlefield of the Mind

Tell Them I Love Them

Peace

The Root of Rejection

Beauty for Ashes

If Not for the Grace of God

By Dave Meyer
Nuggets of Life

Harrison House
Tulsa, Oklahoma 74153

The Harrison House Vision

Proclaiming the truth and the power
Of the Gospel of Jesus Christ
With excellence;

Challenging Christians to
Live victoriously,
Grow spiritually,
Know God intimately.